STEEL
BY LEE MATTINSON

Steel was first performed at Theatre by the Lake, Keswick, on 3 October 2024 followed by a UK tour to The Centre, Maryport, The Beggar's Theatre, Millom, Florence Arts Centre, Egremont, Carlisle Youth Zone and The Carnegie Theatre & Arts Centre, Workington.

STEEL

Cast
Kamran — Suraj Shah
James — Jordan Tweddle

Creative Team
Director — Liz Stevenson
Designer — Simon Kenny
Composer & Sound Designer — Mark Melville
Lighting Designer — Jessie Addinall
Movement Director — Kieran Sheehan
Assistant Director — Mark Macey
Community Choir
  Musical Director — Colin Brind
Scenic Floor Illustrator — Emily Ford

Production Team
Producer — Jamie Walsh
Production Manager — Phil Geller
Assistant Production Manager — Helen Hall
Company Stage Manager — Sarah Goodyear
Costume Supervisor — Gemma Reeve

Promotional Photography — Grant Archer

Steel Community Choir
Lesley Askew, Isel Asquith-Vallance, Grace Edgar, Lauren Elliott, Lynda Grisdale, Glenis Holiday, William Hoodless, Janice Houghton, Michael Huit, Holly Hunter, Stephen Hunter, Andrea Jones, David Jones, Katie Key, Matthew Key, Debra Knight, Pauline McNab, James Mossop, Pat Nelson, Ali Philips, Jennie Rankin, Emily Roper, Bruce Stephens, Carol Telford, Mark Topping, Bethany Webb, Laurence Weldon and Linda Wilkinson.

Cast

Suraj Shah | Kamran

Suraj Shah is an actor originally from Leicester, now based in London. He trained at Mountview Academy of Theatre Arts. His approach to acting is rooted in connecting with audiences, drawing on his rich cultural background and experiences. *Steel* is Suraj's professional theatre debut.

Jordan Tweddle | James

Jordan Tweddle is an award-winning British actor from Wigton, Cumbria. Jordan trained at the Manchester School of Theatre, and since graduating he has worked consistently in television, film and theatre. He is most notably known for his role of Zac Mayers in ITV's *Coronation Street*. In 2019, he was awarded Best Actor at both the Top Indie Film Awards and Monkey Bread Tree Film Awards for his role of Jack in Peccadillo Pictures' *Don't Blame Jack for Boys on Film 20: Heaven Can Wait*. Jordan was recently awarded the ADHD Comedy Award at Edinburgh Fringe for his role of *Pillock*, in his one man show of the same name.

His credits include: *Pillock* (Shakespeare North/Contact Theatre/Edinburgh Fringe); *The BBC's First Homosexual* (BBC and Inkbrew Productions); *Coronation Street* (ITV); *The Looks Department* (Reallife Theatre Company and 53two); *Wings, Lemons Lemons Lemons Lemons Lemons* (Theatre by the Lake); *White Bean Tapas and Manchego* (Qweerdog Theatre); *Don't Blame Jack and Boys on Film: 20* (Peccadillo Pictures), *Love-Pit Potion* (BFI); *No Traveller Returns* (Iron Pier Films); *Frozen* (UK Tour); *Namely, Homely, Comely, Timely* (Whitworth Gallery); *Canopy of Stars* (Tristan Bates Theatre); and *Man of Mode* (HOME).

Creatives

Lee Mattinson | Writer

Theatre credits include: *Crocodiles* (Royal Exchange); *Snap* (Young Vic); *Gary Lineker is Gay* (Paines Plough); *Chalet Lines* (Bush Theatre); *No Wire Hangers* (Soho Theatre); *The Kids Are Alright, I Heart Catherine Pistachio* (Encounter); *Me and Cilla, Jonathan Likes This* (Live Theatre); *The Season Ticket* (Pilot Theatre/Northern Stage). Radio credits include: *Me and Cilla, Tongue, Glow in the Dark, 2 Clowns 1 Trumpet* (BBC Radio 3); *Magpie* (BBC Radio 4); *Prom, Snowglobe* (BBC Radio Newcastle). TV credits include: *Coronation Street* (Story Associate, ITV); *Scallywagga* (BBC 3). Film credits include: *Fist* (Elevator/BFI Network).

Liz Stevenson | Director

Liz is Artistic Director and joint CEO of Theatre by the Lake. Liz was formerly the co-founder and Artistic Director of Junction 8 Theatre. She is a recipient of the JMK Award and directed *Barbarians* at the Young Vic, which was nominated for an Olivier Award .

Other directing credits include: *Brassed Off* (Theatre By The Lake/Octagon Theatre Bolton/Stephen Joseph Theatre); *A Little Princess, Every Brilliant Thing, The Beauty Queen of Leenane, Tom's Midnight Garden, Handbagged* (Theatre by the Lake); *Home, I'm Darling* (Theatre by the Lake/Stephen Joseph Theatre/Octagon Theatre Bolton); *A Christmas Carol* (Theatr Clwyd); *Lancastrians, Under the Market Roof* (Junction 8 Theatre); *The Secret Garden* (York Theatre Royal/Theatre by the Lake); *How My Light is Spent* (Royal Exchange Theatre/Sherman Theatre/Theatre by the Lake); *Macbeth* (Dukes Theatre, Lancaster).

Simon Kenny | Designer

Theatre includes: *Brassed Off* (Theatre by the Lake/Stephen Joseph Theatre/Octagon Theatre Bolton);

The Real & Imagined History of The Elephant Man (Nottingham Playhouse); *Murder in the Dark* (Original Theatre); *Family Tree* (Actors Touring Company); *Duet For One* (Orange Tree); *Blue/Orange* (Royal & Derngate Northampton); *Nothello* (Belgrade/Coventry City of Culture); *The Art of Illusion, The Death of a Black Man* (Hampstead); *Footfalls and Rockaby* (Jermyn Street); several UK tours for Eclipse including *The Gift* (Stratford East) and *Black Men Walking* (Royal Exchange); *Crongton Knights, Noughts & Crosses* (Pilot/UK tours); *Red Dust Road* (National Theatre of Scotland); *Giraffes Can't Dance* (Curve); *The Children* (English Theatre Frankfurt); *Holes* (Nottingham Playhouse/UK tour); *Rose* (HOME); *Twelfth Night, The Merchant of Venice* (Shakespeare's Globe); *Sleeping Beauty, The Ladykillers* (Watermill); *Ghosts* (Theatr Clwyd); *Island* (National Theatre); and *BORDER FORCE*, an immersive installation/performance/club event for Duckie.

Musical theatre includes *The Lord Of The Rings: A Musical Tale* (Watermill/Chicago Shakespeare Theater); *Whistle Down The Wind* (Watermill); *The Lion* (Southwark Playhouse/Arizona Theatre Company); *The Light in the Piazza* (Royal Academy of Music); *The Wiz* (Hope Mill); *Ghost Quartet* (Boulevard Theatre); *Assassins* (Nottingham Playhouse); the multi award-winning *Sweeney Todd* in a purpose-built pie shop (West End/Off-Broadway); *The Selfish Giant* (West End); *Cabaret* (English Theatre Frankfurt); *The World Goes Round* (Stephen Joseph Theatre); and *Saturday Night Fever* (UK tour).

simonkenny.co.uk

Mark Melville | Composer and Sound Designer

Mark Melville is a composer and sound designer for theatre and film and studied at Leeds Conservatoire. His music and sound design work has been presented across the UK and internationally. Recent projects include: *The Fifth Step* (National Theatre of Scotland/Edinburgh International Festival); *Kin* (Gecko/National Theatre); *Midsummer* (Mercury Theatre); *Romeo and Juliet* (Royal Exchange); *Around the World in 80 Days* (Bolton Octagon); *Love the Sinner* (Vanishing Point); *Exodus, The Panopticon* (National Theatre of Scotland); *They Don't Pay? We Won't Pay!* (Mercury Theatre); *Snow Queen* (Storyhouse); *Flight* (Vox Motus/The Bridge Theatre/Barbican); *The Metamorphosis* (Vanishing Point/Emilia Romagna Teatro, Italy); *A Little Space* (Gecko/Mind The Gap); *The Greatest Play in the History of the World...* (Tara Finney Productions/Royal Exchange/West End/UK Tour); *Frankenstein, Wit, B!rth* (Royal Exchange); *Human Animals, Violence and Son, God Bless the Child* (Royal Court); *1984* (Emilia Romagna Teatro); *Tomorrow* (Vanishing Point/Cena Contemporânea Festival, Brazil/ Brighton Festival/Tramway); *Where Do We Belong?, Where Do We Stand?* (Northern Stage); *Little Gift* (M6 Theatre/ AndyManley); *Road* (Leeds Playhouse); *Charlie Sonata* (Royal Lyceum Theatre); *Wonderland* (Vanishing Point/Napoli Teatro Italia/Edinburgh International Festival).

Jessie Addinall | Lighting Designer

Jessie is a Hull based lighting designer. They are also associate lighting designer for *The Roaring Girls* and was an ALPD Lumiere (2020).

Some of their credits include: *GUTS! The Musical* (Hull Truck Theatre); *Baby He Loves You* (Middle Child); *La Scala di Seta* (RNCM); *Snowmen* (The Herd); *Pinocchio* (Hull Truck); *These Majestic Creatures* (Stephen Joseph Theatre); *Romeo and Juliet, As You Like It* (Leeds Conservatoire); *We Could All Be Perfect* (Sheffield Theatres); *Modest* (Middle Child & Milk Presents); *Brief Encounter* (The New Wolsey & Salisbury Playhouse); *Children of the Night* (CAST);

Ladies Day (The New Vic & The Octagon Theatre); *Jack, Mum and The Beanstalk* (Hull Truck Theatre); *Macbeth*, *Twelfth Night* (Leeds Conservatoire); *Ladies Unleashed* (Hull Truck Theatre); *The Whispering Jungle* (Concrete Youth); *A Midsummer Night's Dream* (Hull Truck Theatre); *Teechers Leavers 22'* (Hull Truck Theatre); *The Hound of The Baskervilles* (ERT Theatre); *we used to be closer than this* (Middle Child); *Hull and High Water* (Hull Truck); *Everything I Own* (Hull Truck); *Ducklings* (The Herd); *Beauty Queen of Leenane* (Hull Truck Theatre and Queens Theatre); *The Canary and The Crow* (Middle Child); *Beach Body Ready* (The Roaring Girls); *Paragon Dreams* (Hull Truck); *Us Against Whatever* (Middle Child).

Associate credits include: *Dogs* (Liverpool Playhouse); *71 Coltman Street* (Hull Truck Theatre); *Megalith* (Mechanimal); *Shedding a Skin* (SOHO Theatre).

Kieran Sheehan | Movement Director

Kieran has worked as a movement artist over the last twenty years collaborating on many different kinds of projects and productions; he is currently Associate Director of theatre company Silent Uproar. Kieran develops research projects using movement and often writes and performs about this. Kieran is very proud to be the co-director of Everyone Here whose creative programme is led and shaped by a citizens panel known as Jury for Joy, based in West Cumbria.

Mark Macey | Assistant Director

Mark Macey (they/them) is an American theatre-maker living and working in the UK. Previously they served as Executive Artistic Director of Stage East, a community theatre on the coast of Maine, USA. A graduate of Dell'Arte International's Professional Training Program, Mark is currently pursuing an MFA in Theatre Directing from the University of London, Birkbeck.

THEATRE BY THE LAKE

At our home in the Lake District and out across Cumbria, Theatre by the Lake produces and presents nationally acclaimed theatre, made with passion, that is seen by audiences from across the globe.

We believe that theatre has the power to transform lives and we create vital opportunities for Cumbrian artists, young people and communities to come together, be inspired and explore their creativity.

From our origins as 'The Blue Box', our theatre was willed into existence by the local community and opened by Dame Judi Dench in 1999. 25 years later, under the co-leadership of Artistic Director, Liz Stevenson and Executive Director, Simon Stephens, we continue to be inspired by our unique place and its extraordinary people.

'Artistically sharp and stunningly situated' **New Statesman**

Theatre by the Lake (as Cumbria Theatre Trust) is a registered charity, number 516673.

This production is dedicated to the memory of Casi Clark.

We are thankful for the generous support of
The late Jim Askew
David and Sue Thomas

With thanks to
Anti Racist Cumbria and their young people Ainka, Andreina, Charles, Janice and Millie
The pupils at Workington Academy, West Lakes Academy, Keswick School and the young artists of Kirkgate Youth Theatre
Suzanne Bell
Lee Corner

Steel was developed with the support of the National Theatre's Generate programme.

The Generate Programme

Theatre by the Lake Staff, Trustees and Volunteers

PRESIDENT
Dame Judi Dench

PATRONS
Lord Bragg of Wigton
Sir Tony Cunningham
Mr Hunter Davies OBE
Mr Eric Robson OBE
Dame Patricia Routledge DBE
Mr Richard Wilson OBE

BOARD OF TRUSTEES
Charles Carter (Chair)
Steve Freeman
Elizabeth Freestone
Janaki Fryer-Spedding
Fiona Lowry
Kate McLaughlin-Flynn (Vice Chair)
Phil Moorhouse
Jenna Omeltschenko

LEADERSHIP
Liz Stevenson – Artistic Director and joint CEO
Simon Stephens – Executive Director and joint CEO

FINANCE & ADMINISTRATION
Amanda Leader – Head of Finance & Operations
Luke Robinson – Facilities & Maintenance Manager
Alex Lehninger – Finance Assistant
Carly Picken – General Assistant

ARTISTIC
Amy Clewes – Producer
Claire Dunk – Assistant Producer
Claire Williams – Community Engagement Manager
Sophie Acreman – Company Manager

CUSTOMER EXPERIENCE
Mary Elliott – Customer Experience Manager
Timi Vizmathy – Deputy Customer Experience Manager
Jo Mills – Customer Experience Supervisor
Sarah Graham – Customer Experience Advisor
David Vere-Hoose – Customer Experience Advisor (FOH)
Guy Iozzi – Customer Experience Advisor
James Last – Customer Experience Advisor
Nina Berry – Exhibition Host
Naomi Frost – Exhibition Host

MARKETING
Shelly Ramsdale – Head of Marketing & Communications
Rachel Kearns – Marketing Manager
Rachel Price – Marketing Officer
Caroline Ulyatt – CRM Officer

PRODUCTION
Phil Geller – Head of Production
Symon Culpan – Technical Manager
Gemma Reeve – Wardrobe Supervisor
Louls Ward – Senior Sound Technician
Robert Bullen – Senior Lighting Technician
Daymon Johnstone – Technician
Lizzie Ulyatt – Production Technician
Jester Fyfe – Technician

THANK YOU TO ALL 180 OF OUR VOLUNTEERS
To find out how you can support us visit
theatrebythelake.com/support-us

STEEL

Lee Mattinson

To Mike

With Thanks to

The pupils at Workington Academy, West Lakes Academy, Keswick School and the young artists of Kirkgate Youth Theatre.

Janett Walker and Erika Ghinelli at Anti Racist Cumbria for helping me deliver a series of workshops with their young people and Ainka, Andreina, Charles, Janice and Millie for their invaluable contribution to the lives and ideas of the play.

The Community Choir for co-creating the song for the finale: Lesley Askew, Isel Asquith-Vallance, Grace Edgar, Lauren Elliott, Lynda Grisdale, Glenis Holiday, William Hoodless, Janice Houghton, Michael Huit, Holly Hunter, Stephen Hunter, Andrea Jones, David Jones, Katie Key, Matthew Key, Debra Knight, Pauline McNab, James Mossop, Pat Nelson, Ali Philips, Jennie Rankin, Emily Roper, Bruce Stephens, Carol Telford, Mark Topping, Bethany Webb, Laurence Weldon and Linda Wilkinson.

National Theatre Studio and everyone at the Carnegie Theatre & Arts Centre.

Katie Posner, Akshay Shah, Colin Brind, Cooper McDonough, Louie Ingham, Jill Gordon, Ann Macdonald, David & Sue Thomas and Jim Askew.

And to Rich Henderson, always, for solving the mystery of love.

L.M.

Characters

JAMES
KAMRAN
MARC
LYNN
NICK
WENDY
GWEN
TED
SAM
AARON
GITA

Notes on the Text

This should be achieved with two actors with the following doubling:

Actor 1 James
Actor 2 Everyone Else

Dialogue in **bold** denotes the role-playing of a memory.

This text went to press before the end of rehearsals and so may differ slightly from the play as performed.

After midnight. The steps of St. John's Church. Workington.

JAMES (*seventeen*) *stands and stares at a microphone, top step, centre.*

KAMRAN (*seventeen*) *loiters at the back of the portico, unseen by* JAMES.

JAMES (*into mic*). I reckon the best spot to start's…

Suppose…

(*To himself.*) Think…

KAMRAN. Burger King.

JAMES *turns and clocks* KAMRAN.

KAMRAN. Salterbeck kiss.

JAMES. Course.

I thought you'd gone.

KAMRAN. Come back, didn't I?

JAMES. They can't hear you.

KAMRAN *joins* JAMES *at the microphone.*

KAMRAN (*into mic, loud*). I come back.

JAMES. There's no need to shout.

They look at one another. Awkward.

JAMES (*into mic*). It started with a Salterbeck kiss.

KAMRAN (*into mic*). Means headbutt.

JAMES (*into mic*). Up Distington Burger King.

JAMES *stares out. Freezes.* KAMRAN *flicks* JAMES*'s arm.*

KAMRAN. And?

JAMES. Nervous.

KAMRAN (*into mic*). I dunno if you know Burger King but we do burgers. Shakes. Crispy Chicken Tenders.

JAMES (*into mic, loud*). Whoppers.

We work there.

KAMRAN. *Worked* there. Past tense.

JAMES. Zero-hour contracts.

KAMRAN. We're mostly 'out back'.

JAMES. I'm not allowed around food.

KAMRAN. How many times you failed that food hygiene now?

JAMES. Six. And eleven.

KAMRAN. Seventeen. So I'm mostly shadowing him 'out back'.

JAMES. Meaning cleaning toilets.

KAMRAN. Exactly where we were when it started.

JAMES. The best spot to start.

KAMRAN. The only spot to start.

They both can't help but swap a small smile.

JAMES. **19:10.**

KAMRAN. The time not the year.

JAMES. This one lad's been headbutted.

KAMRAN. Salterbeck kissed by some other lad in the lad's bogs.

JAMES. 'Bloodbath', reportedly.

KAMRAN. Which it's not.

JAMES. There's just a bit of nosebleed by the bin.

KAMRAN. I mop it up.

JAMES. Me sitting watching in the sink.

KAMRAN. It's total silence.

JAMES. Kamran's not talking to me.

KAMRAN. Tell them why.

JAMES. Doesn't matter.

KAMRAN. Dare you.

JAMES. No.

When in comes my dad.

KAMRAN. Absolute first.

JAMES. Too far out of his way.

KAMRAN. Plus he only really eats pizzas.

JAMES. He kicks the 'Cleaning in Progress' sign clean off its hinges.

KAMRAN. Retches at the stench of the bleach.

JAMES. I slip out the sink and stand to attention.

KAMRAN. His dad leans against the hand dryer. Activates it. Shits himself.

JAMES. Stares me up and down and says…

Be him then.

KAMRAN. Why?

JAMES. Cos it's quicker.

KAMRAN. Than what?

JAMES. This. He waits for the dryer to finish and says…

MARC. **James?**

JAMES. Lower.

MARC (*lower*). **James?**

JAMES. **What, Dad?**

MARC. **Listen, lad.**

JAMES. He's pissed.

MARC (*slurs*). **Some snooty lass has left a message on the house phone answerphone for you.**

JAMES. **And you've come all this way to tell me? Must be important. Wanting what?**

MARC. **Asking you to call her.**

JAMES. He hacks up a phlegm and lands it by his bucket.

KAMRAN. Barely missing my trainers.

JAMES. Show them.

KAMRAN. No.

JAMES. **Did she say owt else, Dad?**

MARC. **She did. That there's some sorta money going owing.**

JAMES. **For me?**

MARC. **Aye. Summat to do with the steelworks. With an ancestor on your mam's side. George.**

JAMES. **How much?**

MARC. **A million.**

JAMES. **Bollocks.**

KAMRAN. He turns from James to me and he stares.

JAMES. I've told you, he's pissed.

KAMRAN. Nowt out of the ordinary. But tonight I dare to match it. Stare back.

Knowing how his wad of phlegm was likely meant for me.

JAMES. He's got sinuses.

KAMRAN. He does it all the time.

JAMES. Gob at you?

KAMRAN. Remind me this is his town. His territory. Taken.

JAMES. We watch him leave. Dad. Neither knowing what to say.

KAMRAN. I wasn't talking to you, remember?

JAMES. Dad's always coming out with some shite but this… even for him.

KAMRAN. Was to tell you after work to find a new best mate. Wish I had now.

JAMES. When in comes Chris. Manager. He says…

KAMRAN. 'There's a call for you… some snooty lass.'

JAMES. **19:20.** I find him round the back, swilling out his bucket at the drain.

We're finishing early. Move it.

KAMRAN. **What about my anorak?**

JAMES. **Where we're going we don't need anoraks.**

KAMRAN. **I ask him if he means abroad. He doesn't say.**

JAMES. **Not a word.**

KAMRAN. **Says nowt till we're both on the bus down to town.**

JAMES. **19:22.**

KAMRAN. **Well? What did Snooty McSnoot want?**

JAMES. **Lynn. Likely short for Linda. She didn't fully say.**

KAMRAN. **What *did* she say?** Tell them.

JAMES. That my Great-great-great-grandad George – who I can't remember ever even meeting – owns a mile of British railway track.

KAMRAN. And has done for over a hundred year.

JAMES. A mile they want back.

KAMRAN. James went white.

JAMES. My kegs went brown. **I can't believe it.**

KAMRAN. **What you gonna do?**

JAMES. **What're *we* gonna do? I need you now more than ever. Do this one little thing for me and I'll never ask nowt of you never again.**

KAMRAN. **How is it 'one little thing'?**

JAMES. **By being tiny. You can do what you want when it comes to being mates –**

KAMRAN. **I know I can –**

JAMES. **I'm saying you can, Kamran. But just help me meet her.**

KAMRAN. **Who?**

JAMES. **Linda. Lynn. Ten minutes. In how many years?**

KAMRAN. **Eleven.**

JAMES. **Cos I'm already confused. Please.**

KAMRAN. I thought.

JAMES. For what felt like eleven more years. **Please.**

KAMRAN. **Where you meeting her?**

JAMES. **Butterflies Café.**

KAMRAN. **Don't they shut at six?**

JAMES. **Nine now. They're 'diversifying into tapas'.**

KAMRAN. **Who says?**

JAMES. **Lynn says. Where's tapas? French?**

KAMRAN. **Can't remember.**

JAMES. **I barely understood her on the phone. I think she's the most middle class thing I've ever interacted with.**

KAMRAN. **What about that time you had a Toblerone?**

JAMES. **See? I need you.**

KAMRAN. **Ten minutes.**

JAMES. **Max. So?**

KAMRAN. **The first rule of any negotiation.**

JAMES. **I'm both ears.**

KAMRAN. **Position yourself as an equal. She can't think she's above you.**

JAMES. **Right.**

KAMRAN. **Socially, emotionally, intellectually.**

JAMES. **Easy. How?**

KAMRAN. **Think of ten really middle class things.**

JAMES. **Done. And?**

KAMRAN. **Mention them all.**

JAMES. **Genius.** (*Thinks.*) **Like yoghurt?**

KAMRAN. **Think classier, think…** (*Posh.*) **Waitrose.**

    Think Wimbledon.

    Gout.

    Princess Michael of Kent.

    Deck shoes.

    Mushroom risotto.

    A bonobo monkey.

    Inheritance tax.

    A cockapoo.

    And grapes.

JAMES. **Got it.** Will you pretend to be her, too?

KAMRAN. I wasn't there.

JAMES. So? I told you what happened. I think it'd help and you know you love doing her… no one does Lynn like you do Lynn… even Lynn…

KAMRAN *thinks and playfully assumes the physicality of* LYNN.

KAMRAN (*posh*). Very well.

JAMES. Butterflies. **19:49** and I knew it was her straight off. (*Posh.*) **Lynn?**

LYNN. **James?**

JAMES (*posh*). **Guilty.**

LYNN. **Wow. You sound infinitely scruffier on the telephone.**

JAMES (*posh*). **Do I?**

LYNN. **No offence.**

JAMES (*posh*). **None taken. You look…** (*Thinks.*) **bloody spiffing.**

LYNN. **Thanks. Tapas?**

JAMES (*thinks, French*). **Non. Merci. Madamoiselle.** [No. Thank you. Lady.]

LYNN. **Fabuleux. Tu parles Français. Ça m'étonne – je ne sais pas pourquoi. As-tu été à Paris?** [Fabulous. You speak French. I'm surprised – I don't know why. Have you been to Paris?]

JAMES (*thinks, posh*). **I like Paris. I do. But one does prefer Wimbledon.**

LYNN. **Preach.**

JAMES (*posh*). **And is your Ladyship to be dining this evening?**

LYNN. **One can't eat outside of the M25. She bloats.**

Sorry?

JAMES (*posh*). **I didn't say anything.**

LYNN. **I'm a big fan of these colourful tracksuit bottoms by the way. H&M?**

JAMES (*posh*). **Gout Fashion Week.**

LYNN. Can I get them to get you something? Flat White... Tizer... I saw a Cumberland Sausage Enchilada fly by that looked particularly... (*Thinks.*) brown.

JAMES (*posh*). Unfortunately, I've just had a pint of mushroom risotto.

LYNN. Hilarious.

JAMES (*posh*). I'll tell you what is hilarious, Lynn – a bonobo monkey in deck shoes.

LYNN. Do you mind if I cut straight to the chase, James?

JAMES (*posh*). You sound like Princess Michael of Kent.

LYNN. And for that I apologise. But I need you to focus, okay?

JAMES (*posh*). Grapes.

LYNN. Great. As I said on the telephone we have a situation whereby you – as next of kin to one George Ian McDonough – are in potential possession of a British Rail Mile.

JAMES (*posh*). Inheritance tax.

LYNN. Sort of. I say 'potential' for the following reasons, are you with me?

JAMES (*posh*). Like a cockapoo in Waitrose.

LYNN. Cool.

JAMES (*posh*). Cool.

LYNN. In 1903, George was employed by Moss Bay Steelworks here in Workington. A bumper year by anyone's standards, all core staff were offered one of two Christmas bonuses.

An additional pound in their end-of-year pay packet or one steel mile of that year's spoils. Are you with me?

JAMES (*posh*). Indeed I am.

LYNN. **The steel was only ever a joke, of course. A pound in those days was equivalent to approximately one hundred and twenty today. To which only one silly sausage said, no.**

JAMES (*posh*). **George.**

LYNN. **He requested a contract detailing its transfer of ownership and was invited to head office to accept it. Such was the hoo-ha, he's photographed beneath the wrought iron roof of Euston Station in March of 1904. His smile as wide as his mile, and tickled pink.**

Worthless, London and North Western assumed. A novelty. An idiot. Until earlier this year, his photograph was found in National Archives and, with it, a draft of his contract attached. Which brings me to you today.

JAMES (*posh*). **How so why?**

LYNN. **It indicates, should the original exist, that it satisfies the five required elements to render it legally binding. Who knew?**

JAMES (*posh*). **George. The clever fucking sausage.**

JAMES *laughs haughtily.*

LYNN. **I'm assuming this is news to you. Is it? You can drop the accent.**

JAMES. **There was talk.**

LYNN. **Go on.**

JAMES. **From my nana and my mam. A family joke at best. Of an uncle who once rolled steel into gold.**

LYNN. **Perhaps if I could speak to mum?**

JAMES. **She died.**

LYNN. **Soz. When?**

JAMES. **I was six. Where's his photo?**

LYNN. **Head office.**

JAMES. **And the contract draft?**

LYNN. **My hotel room.**

JAMES. **You're worried I've got the original.**

LYNN. **I wouldn't say 'worried'.**

JAMES. **What would you say, Lynn?**

LYNN. **Curious.**

JAMES. **Is it really worth a million?**

LYNN. **Do you have it or not?**

JAMES nods.

JAMES. **I'll bring you it. Where you staying?**

LYNN. **The Washington Central.**

JAMES. **When by?**

LYNN. **Therein lies the snag. You see, it really did take us months to track you mischievous McDonough boys down.**

JAMES. **When?**

LYNN. **Tomorrow. We're on an eight a.m. deadline.**

JAMES. **If I don't?**

LYNN. **Ownership reverts to Network Rail.**

JAMES. **I bet it fucking does. You think I've not got it.**

LYNN. **I know you haven't.**

JAMES. **Wanna bet?**

LYNN. **I bet you one million pounds you neither have it nor find it in the next twelve hours.**

JAMES. **Deal.** Meanwhile outside. **19:56.**

KAMRAN. **That was sixteen minutes.**

JAMES. **Do you not wanna know what she said?**

KAMRAN. **I want my anorak back. Did she buy it?**

JAMES. **Did she hell. I've till eight in the morning to prove her wrong. To prove I'm not everything I absolutely am. I know.** (*Shouts.*) **Fuck.**

I had nowt then. Less than. In the cold outside Butterflies.

KAMRAN. Kicking the curb to stay warm. **I wish I could help you.**

JAMES. **Why can't you?**

KAMRAN *turns and walks away.* JAMES *stops him with –*

You know I can't do it without you.

Let's at least go out with a bang.

Don't give up on me yet.

KAMRAN. I turned around, didn't I? Stayed.

JAMES *nods.*

I shouldn't've come back. Tonight was your night.

JAMES. Most of which I can't remember.

KAMRAN. It was four hours ago.

JAMES. Help me tell the rest of it.

I remember you not talking to me.

Remember finding out why you weren't.

I remember the hotel room.

Stay.

KAMRAN. And you'll tell them the truth?

JAMES (*thinks, into mic*). Nothing but.

(*Louder.*) As god is my witness.

(*Louder.*) Give it half an hour and we'll all know why you hate me.

(*Louder.*) James McDonough.

(*Louder.*) The million-quid kid.

JAMES *takes a bow and salutes.*

Well?

KAMRAN. **20:00.** And south we head to Salterbeck.

JAMES. Me and my dad's.

KAMRAN. 40 Holden Road.

JAMES. Where I've never not lived.

KAMRAN. **And you've definitely never seen this contract?**

JAMES. **Never ever.**

KAMRAN. **So why'd you say you had?**

JAMES. **It's my golden ticket, isn't it?**

KAMRAN. **Didn't your dad burn most of your mam's stuff?**

JAMES. **Only her clothes.**

KAMRAN. **And the idea is we'll split it, is it?**

JAMES. **No. But I'll not see you wanting.**

KAMRAN. **I want half.**

JAMES. **Then I might see you wanting.**

20:21 and my dad's still out. **Mad Friday, isn't it? End of the month pay day.**

KAMRAN. **He doesn't work.**

JAMES. **He can still observe it.**

KAMRAN. **Where we starting?**

JAMES. We start in the loft where I know he's not been since she died.

KAMRAN. **How's his drinking?**

JAMES. **He could probably go pro.**

KAMRAN. **And he's still really only eating pizzas?**

JAMES. **Like a middle-aged Mutant Ninja Turtle.**

We kick aside a Christmas tree.

KAMRAN. Find piles of old clothes and carrier bags of books.

JAMES. **What'll it look like?**

KAMRAN. **The contract? Paper. Rectangle. Written on. Look for 1904 and his name.**

JAMES. **George Ian McDonough.**

KAMRAN. **If it's legal he'll have signed it.**

JAMES. We tiptoe along the rungs of the loft.

KAMRAN. Scour its cubbyholes and back corners.

JAMES. If it's anywhere, it's there.

KAMRAN. We peer in. **What's that?**

JAMES. **His box of redundancy bits.** His watch and mounted rail track.

KAMRAN. A DVD of the history of the steel industry.

JAMES. Like he didn't already know it. *He's* its history.

KAMRAN. We find that last day's *Times & Star*. 31st of August 2006.

JAMES. Both hold it up to what little light there is.

KAMRAN. Watch the last shift of lads up its faded yellowed front.

They take in the photograph.

JAMES. **Your dad looks the double of you there.**

KAMRAN. **Doesn't.**

JAMES. **What's he doing?**

KAMRAN. **Locking up the gates behind them.**

JAMES. **I hate how he's smiling.**

KAMRAN. **He's having his photo taken.**

He took redundancy, too.

JAMES. **At management rates. Wasn't he at Sellafield come Monday?**

KAMRAN. **You sound like your dad.**

JAMES. We fold it away and return to the dark.

KAMRAN. **Have you decided what you'll do with it yet?**

JAMES. **Take it up the Washington Central.**

KAMRAN. **I meant the money.**

JAMES. **I've only known I'm getting it an hour.**

KAMRAN. **Many would've spent it in less.**

JAMES. I stop. Somewhere above my bedroom and Dad's. The soles of both trainers splintered. And a dried-out spider gone gold in the dark.

KAMRAN. **James?**

JAMES. **I'd leave.**

KAMRAN. **The house?**

JAMES. **Workington. Cos what is there to keep anyone here? Me? Nowt.**

KAMRAN (*thinks*). **There's that new cinema.**

JAMES. **Is that what you're stopping for?**

KAMRAN. **You know what I'm stopping for.**

Leave for good or like…?

JAMES. **20:33** and something's suddenly wrong. Do you mind?

KAMRAN. What?

JAMES. Being my dad.

KAMRAN. From when he come in?

JAMES. From when we first heard him. **20:33** and something's suddenly –

MARC (*shouts, slurs*). **Jaaaammees?**

JAMES. We drop to the landing and watch him in the road.

MARC (*shouts*). **You in?**

JAMES. Already wearing a fight.

MARC (*shouts*). **I want you...**

JAMES. Chicago Town Pizza box in one hand and one of its pies in the other. Hair slicked back from a drink thrown over him.

MARC (*shouts*). **Down here now.**

JAMES. We find him at the front door clawing at his boots. I think he thinks he's putting them on.

MARC. **Listen. I've chatted it through with the lads and we're all of us in agreement – that if there is some sorta money owing going – in any way, shape or form relating to those yards.**

JAMES. He clicks on the light.

MARC. **It's rightly only ours.**

JAMES. Bites his pizza.

MARC. **This is broken.**

JAMES. **It's frozen, Dad.** I take it. Lay it on the *Yellow Pages*. He pulls at a takeaway menu trapped in the snap of the letterbox. Stops.

MARC. **That land belongs to us.**

JAMES. **It's not about the land.**

MARC. **Did she say what they're building?**

JAMES. **They're building nowt.**

MARC. **Be another bloody Tesco's.**

If it's not the land, what is it?

JAMES. **George, on my mam's side.**

MARC. **Aye?**

JAMES. **He owns a share of railway.**

MARC. **Built on steel built by me.**

JAMES. **Which is worth a fair bit.**

MARC. **A million. I told you. True?**

JAMES. I nod.

MARC. **Blood money.**

JAMES. He says and clatters back. To where the hall wall meets the door frame and relaxes. Propped up. A sorta scarecrow then.

MARC. **I saw seven lads die one night.**

JAMES. **We know.**

MARC. **Other's lives ruined. Shells of men. It was hot and it was horrible. But this is how it works, the lads have all said. What goes around comes around and this is just that… for all that horror and all that hell… finally… eventually… payback.**

JAMES. He looks again at his pizza.

MARC. **I thought of your mam on the walk back up. The uncle she said rolled steel into gold and thought who's laughing now? Not her. What I need to know is how.**

JAMES. **What?**

MARC. **I go about getting it. When does it come? The cash.**

JAMES. **There's papers they need.**

MARC. **We've a loft full of papers.**

JAMES. **We've looked. It's something of Mam's.**

MARC. **Everything of hers went when she did.**

JAMES. **Everything?**

MARC. **Almost. Wendy might've took a box or two to remember her by.**

JAMES. **Where's she living?**

MARC. **Your Auntie Wendy? Let me think...**

You know I do know actually...

I'll tell you what, why don't I go? You stop here.

JAMES. **Why?**

MARC. **Cos you owe me. And if it's anyone's million, it's mine.**

JAMES. **You were never married. I'm next of kin.**

MARC. **And I'll ring you once I've seen her. Let you know and we can celebrate together. I'll take you for your first pint. Alright?**

JAMES. Kamran clears his throat.

KAMRAN. **No.**

JAMES. He says.

KAMRAN. And he freezes. Ten pints in and half in and half out of his boots, he stops. **Lynn rang James, not you.**

JAMES. I've never seen anyone stand up to Dad.

KAMRAN. **We'll go**, I tell him and watch it sink in. Watch Marc McDonough – widower, smoker, ex-steelworker – stunned.

JAMES. 'Sorry?' Dad says.

KAMRAN. Like if sorry meant 'start fucking running'.

JAMES. He's pissed.

KAMRAN. I scan him. Watch thick man's hands make fists. His pupils tighten for violence. For the thrill of finally giving me what for. Not for saying no.

JAMES. **Kamran's right.**

KAMRAN. For something far louder.

JAMES. **We'll find her.**

KAMRAN. Something far more offensive. Me. And this skin. In his house.

JAMES. **Where's she living?**

MARC. **It's you I blame for this.**

JAMES. He tells Kamran. Criminals, he calls us.

KAMRAN. I dunno why but I wink. Ding.

JAMES. And he absolutely bastard snaps.

KAMRAN. We bolt.

JAMES. We burst onto Salterbeck Oval.

KAMRAN. Scaling hedges, scaling fences, scaling cars.

JAMES. Hear him behind us. Screaming.

KAMRAN. Slurring.

JAMES. Listing all the many ways he plans to one day make us pay.

KAMRAN. Screaming deviant, screaming hacksaw, screaming axe.

JAMES. We dash.

KAMRAN. East to Moorclose Road and along the line.

JAMES. The once Workington to Distington railway.

KAMRAN. Run the length of the spine of the town.

JAMES. It's wall-to-wall dog walkers.

KAMRAN. Through dog shit and Shih Tzus, we run. Until…

JAMES. **21:01** and we stop. Catch our breaths.

KAMRAN. We've come so far as Navvies Bridge by the Derwent.

JAMES. Where we clock Chris Reynolds.

KAMRAN. Owen Foley.

JAMES. Ten or so lads from school.

KAMRAN. Dodging the weather in the shadow of the bridge.

JAMES. Titch. Joe. And some lass I can't place.

KAMRAN. Vicky.

JAMES. Turns out this is where they come to hang out.

KAMRAN. Not that we were ever invited.

JAMES. **This'll be you soon.**

KAMRAN. **How will it?**

JAMES. **Once I'm gone. Angling for an invite to this shit show.**

KAMRAN. **Doubt it.**

JAMES. **Who'll you have as your new best mate?**

KAMRAN. **I won't.**

JAMES. **Look at them. Dancing under a piss-soaked bridge.**

KAMRAN. **I think it's rain.**

JAMES. **Same thing. I hope you like your drum and bass.**

KAMRAN. **It's psychedelic trance.**

JAMES. **I can see you fitting in here. Laughing at their crack. Small-talking Owen's Corsa. Bucking Vicky in its cramped back seat. Pervert.**

KAMRAN. **Don't take your dad out on me.**

JAMES. **I won't miss this.**

KAMRAN. **When were you ever invited?**

JAMES. **When were you?**

Silence.

KAMRAN. **Doesn't your Auntie Wendy have kids?**

JAMES. **Three grown-up lads now, aye.**

KAMRAN. **Why don't we try town? It's Mad Friday. Everyone's out.**

JAMES. **21:08.** Pub one. 'Spoons and I dunno where to look.

When I last saw my cousins I was six so I'm scanning faces – red from drink and plastered with beards – for the boys hiding inside them – for lads fast-tracked to men on a diet of Fred Perry, Fosters and protein powder.

A bride dashes past in tatters, followed by the Phantom of the Opera, zombie Princess Diana and the American Werewolf from London.

Someone's nana dances.

And a lass I know from school necks a pint of green skittles in a shoulder-to-shoulder circle of lads – her left heel snapped and a sash across her chest – Baby on Board – blue for a boy.

KAMRAN. **Look.**

JAMES. **What?** He points out a gap at the glass-wash end of the bar.

KAMRAN. **Get a better view from there.**

JAMES. Pulls me towards it with my zip.

KAMRAN. And we stop – Shania Twain playing – and take the place in.

JAMES. **Look at it.**

KAMRAN. Dunkirk in double denim. **Do you wanna hurry up?**

JAMES. I'm back to scanning faces.

KAMRAN. When this lad climbs the bar top in front of us.

JAMES. Tight white shirt and tiger-slashed jeans.

KAMRAN. Broad as he is tall.

JAMES. Scores of dirty pint pots at his feet.

KAMRAN. Folk go wild. **What's he doing?**

JAMES. **Dunno.** Till he stares down into my soul. Kicks glasses at the crowd. And I can't work out if he wants to fight me or fuck me.

KAMRAN. Next.

JAMES. **21:15.** Pub four.

KAMRAN. **Anyone who could be them?**

JAMES. **Can't see.**

KAMRAN. I nod at some stairs by the DJ box. **Try higher?**

JAMES. But we can honestly barely move.

KAMRAN. It's ten-at-least deep at the bar and little to no floor left to dance.

JAMES. **Come on.**

KAMRAN. I'm plummeted into people. Into aftershave and Avon. Spray tan. Gum. I tell him it's **like the end of** *Titanic*.

JAMES. **Can't hear you.**

KAMRAN (*louder*). **If Leo had his eyebrow pierced and Winslet was a jam eater –**

JAMES (*louder*). **What?**

KAMRAN (*louder*). **Which is actually really funny cos I dunno if you know but** *Titanic* **was directed by Academy Award Winner James Cameron which is mine and your names as one uniquely talented man.**

JAMES (*louder*). **Go faster.**

KAMRAN (*louder*). **How, when no one's moving?** A tall lass snogs a short lad right in front of us and split.

JAMES. Wriggling towards the DJ. **Keep going.**

KAMRAN. **I'm trying.** I don't say it but think it.

JAMES. What?

KAMRAN. How different folk react.

JAMES. To what?

KAMRAN. Us. You, they make space for. Me? Concrete.

JAMES. **Mad Friday, what do you expect?**

KAMRAN. Not this. They're on my feet, they're in my pockets, **get off. Aye, I mean you.** One lad howls so loud in my face, I swear I smell the corners of his lungs. **Move it.**

JAMES. We hit the stairs.

KAMRAN. You before me and look out across the pub. **Owt?**

JAMES. **Nowt.** We minesweep a pint each.

KAMRAN. Means 'nick it'.

JAMES. We nick a pint each. Neck a pint each.

KAMRAN. And leave through the piss-flooded bogs.

JAMES. **21:22.** Pub seven.

KAMRAN. **Tell me what they look like and I'll find them myself.**

JAMES. **I've told you, I was six.**

KAMRAN. *One* **distinguishing feature. A moustache… a hat… bald.**

JAMES (*thinks*). **I mean…**

KAMRAN. **There's a million in it, remember?**

JAMES (*thinks*). **One of them… might've been…**

(*Thinks.*) **Definitely, potentially…**

(*Thinks.*) **Some sort of ginger-haired gentleman?**

KAMRAN. **James McDonough: Memory Man.**

JAMES. You do this next bit.

KAMRAN. The pub's called Gaslight. Time?

JAMES. **21:24.**

KAMRAN. And wall-to-wall with lads.

JAMES. You're looking at two hundred-odd lads.

KAMRAN. All in the same white T-shirt, skinny jeans, Converse High Tops.

JAMES. Hair slicked up and left ears pierced.

KAMRAN. Photocopies of photocopies of photocopies of lads.

JAMES. **Be you one day.**

KAMRAN. I watch a sea of faces as white as their tops. **Doubt it.**

JAMES. I point out a ginger in the corner by the plasma.

KAMRAN. Chugging a bottle of Blossom Hill red.

JAMES. **Told you.** That's him – Nick. When all hell breaks loose.

KAMRAN. Cos before we can move some young lad's hit.

Takes a glass to the back of his head for dancing to Rihanna.

JAMES. **Shit.**

KAMRAN. And he's kicked through a padlocked fire door fast.

Down some stairs and through some gates.

We're forced out after him as lads take turns.

Where blood ruins T-shirts.

Bright white Topman en masse, wrecked.

His face unrecognisable.

Teeth out, earring out, his panicked breaths brown the air and so much blood we watch a drain get blocked. Two drains. Three.

With all in attendance in agreement that he asked for it. The puff on the ground. Grit in his wounds. And all the Rihanna fan he ever was. His dancing now writhing, now broken, now pain.

JAMES. **21:25. Look.**

KAMRAN. I expect his cousin. **What?**

JAMES. **My dad.** Flashing folk my photo from his cracked Motorola.

KAMRAN. **What'll we do?**

JAMES. **Fucking move.** And we're off.

KAMRAN. Rush dim-lit streets behind pubs.

JAMES. By the indoor market where my nana once shopped.

KAMRAN. Find alleyways and ginnels.

JAMES. Cobbles and gates.

KAMRAN. Find old town.

JAMES. Ghost town.

KAMRAN. No one. Stop.

JAMES. **Why you not been talking to me?**

I've not seen you since my birthday.

Is it that?

KAMRAN. **Can I ask you something?**

JAMES. **Not if it's about your anorak.**

KAMRAN. **Do you remember what happened on your birthday?**

Silence. JAMES *shakes his head.*

There he is.

JAMES. **21:28.** (*Shouts.*) **Nick?**

KAMRAN. Annihilated and looking for somewhere to piss.

JAMES. Chips in one hand, his iPhone in the other.

It's James, your cousin, do you remember?

NICK (*tiny*). **Lost.**

JAMES. He unlocks his phone with his face.

NICK (*louder*). **Want Kelly.**

JAMES. Hands it over and I see her as his background.

NICK (*louder*). **Phone home.**

JAMES. **Alright, E.T.**

I ring her and – 'this isn't my Nick,' she says. I hear their baby in the background. *Strictly*. Her opening more crisps. She's lovely. 'Is he okay?'

He's fine. I watch him lose a battle with a sachet of brown sauce and wonder where he went – the father formally known as Nick.

NICK (*tiny*). **Want Kelly.**

JAMES. 'What's he saying?'

That he loves you.

'I'll book him a taxi.'

Where am I sending him?

NICK. **Disneyland.**

JAMES. We make small talk until it arrives and I work out I know Kelly's sister.

The driver says, 'it's a forty quid charge if he spews.'

He's gonna be alright.

You gonna be alright?

NICK. **I miss my Mam.**

JAMES. Nick says. Biting back tears. Six again. **What happened?**

Where's your mam living? We could take you there now, if you like?

He shakes his head, he's done. So I scroll through his unlocked phone and I ring her and ask her myself.

21:39. Wendy's.

WENDY. You know that cat I've been trying to make come into my house and be my best friend?

JAMES. No.

WENDY. It's died. And Nick sends his love, does he?

JAMES. Absolutely.

WENDY. We've not actually spoken in a year. Did he mention that?

JAMES. He didn't.

WENDY. And it's your uncle Tom you're after, is it? Only he's left me, too.

JAMES. It's about my mam.

WENDY. I'll not say who for, but it's the lass from Moss Bay Chinese.

JAMES. Dad said you might've took a box or two of hers when she died.

WENDY. Unless he's sent you? Tom. Your uncle Tom. My Tom, has he?

JAMES. Sorry.

WENDY. That's everyone now. Cider?

JAMES. We're sort of in a rush.

WENDY. I could make you a bacon sandwich? Extra crispy.

JAMES. We're alright.

WENDY. Do you know where he said he was going? Your uncle Tom. My Tom. To cover his tracks.

JAMES. No.

WENDY. A retired steelworker's choir. I leapt. Here's me cheering, knowing how much it'd mean to him. And after so many years on that sofa, sobbing and rotting, I encouraged it – sing, I said.

Cos when they closed those yards, who saved us?
Women. Wives. And what do we get? Left. Shut for good,
ourselves.

JAMES. Dad said you might've took a box or two of my
mam's. Did you?

WENDY. We met at sixteen. 1985. The final day of the
Miner's Strike. Your grandad had us handing out flowers
to the crowd.

JAMES. How come?

WENDY. Carnations were symbols of heroes, he said. We'd
stole a load from someone's garden up Stainburn that
morning. And as soon as Tom took it I knew – knew
instant and infinite love.

JAMES. Sorry.

WENDY. Nick stood by him, of course. Took his side over
mine. Lads and their dads, eh? I said some very ugly
things I... didn't mean.

JAMES. Maybe he misses you, too?

WENDY. Won't do.

JAMES. You've his number now. Ring him. Ask him.

WENDY. He made his bed. Him and Tom, both. You're as
lanky as your grandad, mind, you big, long streak of piss.
Can I hug you?

We had many a cross word across the years, me and your
mam. Hadn't spoken in a long time when she died. I
thought I one day might forgive her.

JAMES. For what?

WENDY. I did take a box. It went to your Uncle Aaron's
when the garage flooded. We're talking a very long time
ago now.

JAMES. I never knew I had an Uncle Aaron.

WENDY. And now you do.

JAMES. **Where's he living?**

WENDY. **Your nana's old flat.**

JAMES. **Newlands Gardens?**

WENDY. **Number seven. Nick's second luckiest number. And he's safe, is he?**

JAMES. **I'm sure he'll be back. I could visit you in the meantime now I know where you are. I love cider and bacon sandwiches.**

WENDY. **You know I don't even know its name. The baby.**

I imagine you do. What is it?

Just say if it's a boy or a girl. Just say.

I've a box room full of stuff for it.

I dunno what to buy, what it likes, what it is. Do you two?

JAMES. I leave her standing staring.

KAMRAN. Glaring at us both.

JAMES. Her mobile goes. She scans its screen.

KAMRAN. Says it's his dad and **better make a move**, we both tell her.

JAMES. She lets it ring.

KAMRAN. Saying she wishes it was Tom. Or Nick. Kelly. Or the cat she's been trying to make come into her house and be her best friend.

JAMES. **21:48.** 7 Newlands Gardens. No answer. (*Shouts.*) **Aaron?**

I tell him through the letterbox who I am and still he uses the stranger chain. **I never knew I had another uncle**. See so much of my mam in what little of his face he allows.

Wendy says you've a box of hers.

Nowt.

Have you?

He nods and looks past me to Kamran – sat on his front wall.

KAMRAN. I tell him someone's spray painted **a massive cock and balls** up the side of his house but he says he's seen it. His upstairs neighbour brays on the window for us to fuck-the-fuck-off and I widen my eyes at James to hurry.

JAMES. **Only there's something I think might be in it. Her stuff. Which is actually life or death, Uncle Aaron. A contract. Between George and… I've forgot who she said but it's old, like dead old, like 1904.**

I dunno if you've ever seen cult classic *The Goonies*?

KAMRAN. Aaron nods.

JAMES. **It's probably like the map off that.**

KAMRAN. He's yet to blink.

JAMES. **I've nothing of hers. My dad torched the lot when she died. So, that aside, I'd be interested in knowing what else there might be… in amongst her things… Wendy never said.**

KAMRAN. He turns away at her name and I try to see past him to the inside of his flat. To what goes on in the dark and with who. To what music. Pictures hanging. Trinkets watching. He blinks and I swear I catch glitter.

JAMES. **Do you know what Wendy couldn't forgive my mam for?**

KAMRAN. And the door's slammed.

JAMES (*shouts*). **Aaron?**

(*Louder.*) **Listen…**

(*Louder.*) **You've always been my favourite uncle, Uncle Aaron.**

I stop. Give up. Shrink back to the lad I was at half seven. To being ignored and having nowt. A Salterbeck kiss. Blood. Bleach.

When something leaves his letterbox and dances down to stone. It's paper so old it could shatter like glass. Numbers nineteen and four stood shoulder to shoulder with a zero. Signed George Ian McDonough.

KAMRAN. **Is that it?**

JAMES. And I grin for fucking Cumbria.

22:00. Washington Central Hotel. Reception.

GWEN. **Good evening, sir, how can I help?**

JAMES. **Alright, Gwen? How's your dad? Still seeing that lollipop lady?**

GWEN. **Good evening, sir, how can I help?**

JAMES. **Yeah, I rang ahead.**

GWEN. **It was me you spoke to, sir.**

JAMES. **Gwen – it's James and Kamran. From school?**

GWEN. **I struggled to decipher precisely what…**

JAMES. **I was running. There's a guest I need to speak to.**

GWEN. **Name?**

JAMES. **James.**

GWEN. **Their name, sir.**

JAMES. **Lynn.**

GWEN. **And can I take a room number from you there, sir?**

JAMES. **That's ideally what I'm looking for from you.**

GWEN. **Guests room numbers are strictly confidential, sir. Something we take very seriously here at the Central.**

JAMES. **Clearly.**

GWEN. **We're not eighty-five pounds plus breakfast per night for nothing.**

JAMES. **Do you remember that time you shit yourself in assembly, Gwen? You weren't this snooty then. Lynn. Is she in?**

GWEN. **Negative.**

JAMES. **Then I'd like her room number and a key card. Pronto. A little packet of Bourbons each to get us up the stairs. And Gwen?**

GWEN. **Sir?**

JAMES. **Ta. 22:04.** Washington Central Penthouse. **Drink it in.**

KAMRAN. **This is living.**

JAMES. **There's a minibar.**

KAMRAN. **Do you want one?**

JAMES. **Vodka. Neat. On the rocks. Lemonade and no ice.**

KAMRAN. **You're even starting to sound like a millionaire.**

JAMES. **When I am, I'm living on Martinis.**

KAMRAN. **Bianco or Rosso?**

JAMES. **Both. Shaken *and* stirred.**

KAMRAN. **Classy.**

JAMES *looks out.*

JAMES. **You can see all the way to the fells from up here. Is that Everest?**

KAMRAN. **Skiddaw.**

JAMES. **How'd you know?**

KAMRAN. **Surrender.**

Surrender.

Heart.

Says.

Go.

JAMES. **Eh?**

KAMRAN. **The Lake District's five highest mountains.**

Surrender. Scafell Pike.

Surrender. Scafell.

Heart. Helvellyn.

Says. Skiddaw.

Go. Great End.

JAMES. What you doing?

KAMRAN. It's called a mnemonic. I'd use them at school to remember stuff, do you not remember?

JAMES. No.

KAMRAN. I had one for the entire periodic table. Will I sing it?

JAMES. Should we both get room service instead?

KAMRAN. Not hungry.

JAMES. Me neither.

KAMRAN. She can't be long.

JAMES. Nervous.

KAMRAN. There's nowhere for her to go.

JAMES. Unless Marks & Spencer's is twenty-four hours?

KAMRAN. It's not.

JAMES. Let's just wait.

They wait.

I'm a big fan of these paintings by the way.

KAMRAN. They're etchings.

JAMES. I might start collecting etchings. What's it meant to be?

KAMRAN. A fox hunt.

JAMES. What's that?

KAMRAN. It's called a valance.

JAMES. Toastie maker?

KAMRAN. Trouser press.

JAMES. And him?

KAMRAN. Just a towel someone's folded into a swan to suggest elegance and grace. Will I move it? We could sit on the bed.

JAMES. Why when I'm happy standing?

They wait.

KAMRAN. How rich do you think Lynn is?

JAMES. Seriously. I'm talking megabucks. Harrods. A cleaner.

KAMRAN. How much per year?

JAMES (*thinks*). Eleven grand.

They wait.

KAMRAN. What if she's ran into your dad?

JAMES. He'll be back down the club by now.

KAMRAN. Can she drink outside of the M25?

JAMES. How would I know?

KAMRAN. Should we check the bar?

JAMES. You go.

KAMRAN. Why?

JAMES. Cos I'm waiting here. Unless you've gotta get off?

KAMRAN. No.

JAMES. Where do your mam and dad think you are?

KAMRAN. Yours, probably. Give her five more minutes and I will.

They wait.

Did I tell you I found porn in his briefcase?

JAMES. You've not been talking to me. Who's, your dad's?

KAMRAN. Nowt weird. Just tits and squirty cream and that. He'd done a serious amount of damage to the front cover.

JAMES. Can you still get it in magazine?

KAMRAN. I think it was an old one.

JAMES. Why?

KAMRAN. She was bent over a fax machine. In a shell suit. Eating Opal Fruits.

JAMES. With squirty cream? Tramp.

KAMRAN. What you gonna do about your dad?

JAMES. He hasn't got a briefcase.

KAMRAN. I meant the money. He thinks it's his.

JAMES. It's not.

KAMRAN. Not all of it.

JAMES. None of it. Can we just... wait?

They wait.

KAMRAN. But folk who worked the steelworks.

JAMES. I don't care.

KAMRAN. Is it not a bit theirs? Those left with nowt when it closed.

JAMES. They didn't have nowt. They had a pound in 1903.

KAMRAN. I dunno if you're being serious or not.

JAMES. It's not my fault their ancestors were idiots.

KAMRAN. Folk can't eat.

JAMES. And what do you think I'm fucking living on?

I don't even know why you're here.

KAMRAN. You were begging me an hour back.

JAMES. For half, if I remember rightly.

KAMRAN. What would George do?

JAMES. What would *you* do?

KAMRAN. Share it.

JAMES. **Liar.**

KAMRAN. Money isn't everything.

JAMES. It is when you've got none.

Silence.

KAMRAN. Do you think your dad really did see seven lads die?

JAMES. Shut up.

Silence.

I've seen the photos of their funerals. He did, aye. Soz.

KAMRAN. How long was he there?

JAMES. He started their general training scheme at sixteen. Worked his way up from stopper boy to the Bessemer, coke ovens, rolling mill, rail bank. It's all he talks about.

KAMRAN. Have you heard of Robert Edwards?

JAMES. Him from Moorclose who pours boiling water over kids?

KAMRAN. That's Edward Roberts. Robert Edwards was a pirate given seventy-seven acres of Manhattan by Queen Anne.

JAMES. What for?

KAMRAN. Disrupting Spanish sea-lanes. He leased it to the Cruger brothers in 1778 with the understanding it'd revert to him once it expired. But the lease agreement was lost. For land worth $650 billion.

JAMES. **What's your point?**

KAMRAN. **That at least you found your treasure. Some folk, most folk, never do. You could've stayed stuck here forever with me.**

JAMES. **If steel's worth a million-a-mile, why they not still making it?**

KAMRAN. **They are. Just not here.**

JAMES. **Where?**

KAMRAN. **When the works first closed – Scunthorpe, France, Poland.**

JAMES. **Where now?**

KAMRAN. **I dunno.**

JAMES. **What does your dad do at Sellafield to warrant a briefcase?**

KAMRAN. **Dunno.**

JAMES. **Can he get my dad a job?**

KAMRAN. **Dunno.**

JAMES. **What do you know?**

KAMRAN. **That your birthday… if I'm never gonna see you again.**

JAMES. **Enough. I'm getting room service.**

KAMRAN. **We should talk about it.**

JAMES. **If I get a burger and a curry will you eat what I don't?**

KAMRAN. **He saw us. Your dad.**

JAMES. **Didn't.**

I've not eaten since yesterday.

And I've told you. Can't remember.

KAMRAN. I'd come round yours to watch a film. Your dad had a do on down the club so we watched it downstairs. Sank the best part of a bottle of Bacardi and started on the sofa as we normally would your bed. Soon found the floor. Trackies off, tops off, kegs off, all.

JAMES. Okay.

KAMRAN. Swapped the film for some music and we're up.

JAMES. Right.

KAMRAN. Pressed against the wall to that album you like to fuck to.

JAMES. Did I even see you on my birthday? (*Thinks.*) Don't think so.

KAMRAN. I don't hear him. If I had, I'd've said. I just turn. I somehow know to and I see him at the living room door. Watching. For I dunno how long. Could've been seconds, could've been…

JAMES. I don't even like Bacardi. What is it?

KAMRAN. I stopped it. Told you I felt funny.

JAMES. You never could handle your drink.

KAMRAN. Asked you to walk me home.

JAMES. Same thing's happening now.

KAMRAN. I wanted you out the house.

JAMES. That pint's gone straight to your head.

KAMRAN. I thought he might kill us.

JAMES. Are you wanting food or not, Kamran?

KAMRAN. 'Walk your fucking self home,' you said.

I told you I loved you.

And 'weak,' you called me. 'Puff.'

JAMES. There's gammon.

KAMRAN. 'Man up,' you said. From a mouth still wet with kisses. I hated you.

JAMES. Do you not think he'd have said?

KAMRAN. He didn't call us criminals earlier.

JAMES. He called us shoplifters.

KAMRAN. Shirtlifters. Old school. He knows.

JAMES. I don't care what he thinks.

KAMRAN. Do you care what I think?

JAMES. No. Nowt here matters now. I've told you, I'm going.

KAMRAN. Without Lynn?

JAMES. She'll be back any minute.

KAMRAN. She's gone. Good luck getting to London for eight a.m.

JAMES. Her stuff's here.

KAMRAN. On eleven grand she can afford more. Congratulations. Fucked it.

KAMRAN *looks out.*

JAMES. I look through her stuff. Find the handwritten copy of George's contract and compare it to mine. Word-for-word. Legit. With it there's a letter instructing me of the deadline. A letter she's kept.

'Failure to provide said contract by zero hundred hours will result in the aforementioned one mile of track being reabsorbed by the whole and thereafter the legal intangible asset of Network Rail.'

LYNN. It would appear the deadline is, in fact, midnight. Oops.

JAMES. She lied.

KAMRAN. Look. Down outside St. John's. Folk are flocking.

JAMES *looks out.*

JAMES. **Is it some sort of riot?**

KAMRAN. **What they saying?**

JAMES. **Listen.**

KAMRAN. Words emerge from the crowd. Float up to the window where, high above the streets, in a Penthouse in the stars we hear…

JAMES. 'James.'

KAMRAN. Hear, 'money,' hear, 'steel.' **They know.**

JAMES. **How?**

KAMRAN. I point out his dad in his work boots from the yards.

JAMES. **He's probably just there cos he's… must've been passing.**

KAMRAN. **Stop making excuses.**

JAMES. **I'm not.**

KAMRAN. **He's there for your money. Cos he's greedy. Like he's racist.**

JAMES. **No.**

KAMRAN. **And not cos he's pissed. Or cos it's Mad Friday. Cos it's his town, his territory, taken.**

JAMES. **You said that.**

KAMRAN. **He says it every time I see him. Written in his pit bull-brown eyes. Marc McDonough – bigot.**

JAMES. **Is this cos I called you a puff? Cos you are. Deal with it.**

KAMRAN. **Why don't you?**

Silence.

Do you think your Uncle Aaron is?

JAMES. **No.**

KAMRAN. You must've seen his nail varnish.

JAMES. I saw them up close and it was muck.

KAMRAN. Muck can shimmer.

And you kissed me, remember? The first time.

I'd've gone to uni and regretted it forever.

JAMES. It's not my fault you failed your exams.

KAMRAN. I never said it was. But you made the move. You pressed play.

JAMES. I don't make excuses cos I think he's right.

KAMRAN. I wish he'd just smash me in the face. At least then I'd know where I stand.

JAMES. He's not like that.

KAMRAN. He chased us up the street screaming deviant, screaming hacksaw, screaming axe.

JAMES. Not cos of that.

KAMRAN. I grieve a life where I wasn't so different. Where I'm enough.

JAMES. I never said you weren't enough.

KAMRAN. You never say nowt and that's the fucking problem.

'Man up.' What's that even mean?

JAMES *shrugs. Silence.*

He called me 'double trouble' once. Your dad. Do you remember?

I was nine and how am I? I thought. What else am I doing wrong?

It was years before I knew. That how I held myself and having a sort of softness meant... different. Meant dangerous. And he'd seen that – warning – not like other lads. Befriend at own risk.

JAMES. Whatever I say, you'll only accuse me of making excuses. So?

KAMRAN. There's joy in being different. I need to run at that. Not you.

JAMES. Loud and clear.

KAMRAN. Battered like steel into shape by your dad.

JAMES. Nice.

KAMRAN. Loves the way to work out who you are. And I have.

JAMES. Congratulations. Beautiful. But I know what you're doing.

KAMRAN. What?

JAMES. You're very clever, Kamran. So let's just call it – what? – five hundred. Cash. To see me over this last little hurdle with Lynn.

KAMRAN. This isn't about the money.

JAMES. And then you can fuck off. I'm not stupid.

There's joy in being different.

But there's more in being rich.

KAMRAN. I didn't know you at all then. You disappeared completely.

JAMES. Tell them what you did.

KAMRAN. I snatched the contract.

JAMES. Kamran.

KAMRAN. Kicked wide the window.

JAMES. You fucking doing?

KAMRAN. And threw it.

JAMES. Dumbstruck, I watched. A kite then, it soared. Higher than the dome of St. John's. Quicker than the crowd until gone. You didn't say a thing.

KAMRAN. I was already at the door. The end.

KAMRAN *makes to leave.*

JAMES. Do you not wanna know where I've been in the two hours since?

KAMRAN. See you, James.

JAMES. The pub by the docks.

KAMRAN *stops.*

KAMRAN. What took you there?

JAMES. I'll tell you. I promised you the truth and you'll get it. As God is my witness but first there was Ted.

KAMRAN *turns.*

KAMRAN. How'd you even know what that is? The pub.

JAMES *nods at the microphone.*

JAMES. **22:16.** You must've seen him. Walked straight past him. Stood on the steps of St. John's… stood at this microphone… Ted said…

KAMRAN *stands at the microphone.*

TED (*into mic*). **Ted Cunningam. Current Allerdale trade union spokesperson and former General Secretary for the Iron and Steel Trades Confederation.**

JAMES. You all went mute.

TED (*into mic*). **What do we know? That Thatcher was a wrecking ball. That she decimated our industry with savage renationalisation. That Workington fell to its knees and never stood up.**

JAMES. I inched my way forward as he spoke.

TED (*into mic*). **What do we know?**

JAMES. **Excuse me.**

TED (*into mic*). **That lady luck has shone a glimmer of hope on our small corner of West Cumbria in the form of a lad. A boy. A whippersnapper with a bolt of lightening in his hands.**

JAMES. I saw my dad handing out flyers.

TED (*into mic*). **But what to do?**

JAMES. Change direction.

TED (*into mic*). **Governed not by memories of long, cold winters with shivering empty stomachs but by right and by wrong. Is it his or rightly ours, this million pound mile of steel? Ay?**

JAMES. **Excuse me.** Scanning all hands for the contract as I pass.

TED (*into mic*). **His father, who I spoke to at length put it best, put it simply, when he said:**

JAMES. When I saw the face on it – the flyer – for the first time – mine.

TED (*into mic*). **'This is for everyone who has ever called here home. Folk forged from the sparks of those yards. For we know what it is to be forced to our knees but today we stood and tonight we rise.'**

JAMES. Ted clocks me. **Shit.** I turn to the crowd, jaws drop and I'm off –

Darting through the graveyard and spilling onto Peter Street –

Roper Street, John Street, Oxford Street, run –

Steelman's, shop fronts, railings and an HSBC –

Folk flying from all angles –

Stretching at and snatching at and grabbing at from cars –

Faster, thinking faster, thinking faster, thinking – bang –

A tin of pop thuds my back –

Bricks arrive –

Bottles arrive –

Owt they've got gets thrown –

Come burgers, come fag ends, come traffic cones –

(*Shouts.*) Be absolutely faster –

(*Louder.*) Past Iceland, Halifax, CeX –

(*Louder.*) Onto Speedwell, Brow Top, Griffin –

(*Louder.*) Bombing through town like a Workington fucking Pac-Man.

22:20. I stop and look. Lost them.

KAMRAN. Where you at?

JAMES. Past Cloffocks. Perry's Palace. Travelodge. Staring up at big Tesco's. It's car park packed with not a single soul in sight.

KAMRAN. What do you do?

JAMES. I walk across the roundabout, hood up, head down and hot-foot it past the lass on fags. There's only staff left. Baskets abandoned. Trolleys strewn.

KAMRAN. What you thinking?

JAMES. How I'm that dehydrated I could drink my own piss.

KAMRAN. Meal-deal fridge?

JAMES. You know those sexy little smoothies we like?

KAMRAN. Pineapple Paradise or Mango Mayhem?

JAMES. One of each and cold to the touch.

KAMRAN. Result.

JAMES. When I see them at my side.

KAMRAN. Who?

JAMES. Sam. Taller than me. Fitted leather jacket with what looks like Tipp-Ex up it's back. **22:26** and they just start talking.

SAM. Alright?

JAMES. **Alright?** You return both smoothies from my hand to the fridge.

KAMRAN. Why?

JAMES. You say it'll rot my teeth.

SAM. **Yeah, you really shouldn't drink these. Admittedly they're astronomically delicious and even better cold but contrary to popular belief they're mostly sugar and will therefore rot every last tooth in that head. I should know, I'm a professional dentist.**

JAMES. You're not even an amateur dentist. You're buying a bottle of water I watch you walk to the self-serve with.

KAMRAN. What's up the back of my jacket?.

JAMES. I don't realise yet.

KAMRAN. And then?

JAMES. The shoplifter buzzer goes. It's Wendy.

WENDY. **What?**

JAMES. Wrestled to the ground by a manager.

WENDY. **So I forget to pay for one little thing and suddenly I'm an opportunistic criminal mastermind, am I?**

JAMES. He relieves her of a bunch of flowers and two children's bikes.

WENDY. **I think you'll find I arrived on those.**

JAMES. She's asked to review the CCTV at the fag counter and pinpoint the moment she rode in on a pink and blue bike.

WENDY. **I'll not say who for, but it's the lass from Moss Bay Chinese.**

JAMES. The leather jacket winks and leaves and…

KAMRAN. What?

JAMES. I follow.

KAMRAN. Why?

JAMES. I turn right and right again to the station. Watch them cross the footbridge as the trains unload below. As platforms fill with talk of St. John's, with directions wanted and justice needed.

'String him up.' 'Rip him limb from limb.' 'What way now, marra?'

From far and wide, they're coming – Maryport, Wigton, Millom.

I stare at the rails and wonder who rolled them. If George or my dad had. If I might've too had the works not closed. Thinking, how might this town have grown? How should it have? If I'd've died there even.

I think of mam. Of the hum steel makes when there's something on it coming and… you and what you'd said… violence, love, shame.

I follow the scent of Tipp-Ex to the west most edge of town. Watch them walk towards a pub where the harbour kisses the sea. Cock and balls up its side and lit up as if for Christmas.

22:38. Pub eight and I dunno where to look.

I'm scanning drag queen's faces – bright from dancing and plastered with make-up – for the boys hiding inside them – for lads fast-tracked to lasses on the maths of Boots No7, CK One and 'Mambo No. 5'.

Sam joins a table of other lasses, all in leather jackets, all with Tipp-Ex up their backs. I see then they're the T-Birds from *Grease*. That everyone's in fancy dress and a banner above the bar says 'fundraiser' – written in rainbow and tied up with string.

Someone's nana dances. Rihanna playing. I take it all in.

When a queen climbs the table in front of me – tight white skirt and tiger-print tights. She stares down into my soul, blows kisses at the crowd and speaks. I know that voice. Uncle Aaron?

AARON. Sorry, darling... have I been sniffing glue or is this... as she lives and bastard breathes, a McDonough she sees before her?

JAMES. I just stare at him... and her... them both.

AARON. Speak, sweet angel. Grace us, like Jesus, with the reason for your coming. Dazzle us with the casualties of another Mad Friday. But first and regrettably foremost, remind me of your name again...?

JAMES. James.

AARON. But in honour of whom? Cook... Brown... and the Giant Peach?

JAMES. Grandad. Your dad.

AARON. God rest it's bigoted soul. Still. Hello-hello-hello, James.

JAMES. Alright-alright-alright? Is it still Uncle Aaron?

AARON. It most certainly is not. For tonight, I am transubstantiated. I am metamorphosed. The very effigy of magnificence, rapture and wit.

JAMES. What do I call you?

AARON. I... for an eye... am Steel Magnolia.

JAMES. Cos your dress is cream?

AARON. This? Is Hitchcock Ivory and, no. In recognition of Dame Shirley MacLaine. You've surely heard of Shirley, James.

Recipient of no less than seven Golden Globes?

Known for her deft portrayal of charming eccentricity?

Star of *Terms of Endearment*, *Some Come Running* and *The Yellow Rolls-Royce*?

JAMES. Is that a film?

AARON. They *all* are films. As is *Steel Magnolias*. Do you even go to school?

JAMES. **I'm seventeen.**

AARON *softens.*

AARON. **I see that. Help Nana...**

AARON *holds out his hand.* JAMES *helps him down from the table.*

And what brings a starlet like you to a hovel like this?

JAMES. **I'm sorta being hunted by the entire town. You?**

He points at the banner above the bar.

AARON. **Fundraising.**

JAMES. **For what?**

AARON. **The pub. They're selling it out from under us.**

JAMES. **There's a hundred other pubs in town.**

AARON. **And we want this one. Centuries old and home to those the town spits out. It's a lighthouse.**

JAMES. **As well as a pub?**

AARON. **Look at you. What I wouldn't give to be seventeen and consumed by curiosity. Stood at the door to opportunity and heartache. To a glittering new world of love and loss and loneliness. Cocktail?**

JAMES. How come you know so much about somewhere you weren't?

KAMRAN. What did you have?

JAMES. Porn Star Martini. It's sorta Vodka-Fanta with a slice of boiled egg.

KAMRAN. Passion fruit.

JAMES. I tell him I'd've preferred a pint and crisps but Diana Ross had already opened the tin. He's says he's sorry about before.

KAMRAN. Round his?

JAMES. Him and his flat mate Greg had had a fight.

KAMRAN. 'Flat mate.' Told you. And then?

JAMES. **I lost the contract, Uncle Aaron. My dad's hell-bent on getting it back. He's had these 'wanted' flyers printed.**

Aaron's not listening. He studies my face. Looks away.

What was my mam like? I was only six when…

I've always wondered why Dad got me and not her.

She must've done something really wrong. Like what Wendy said.

What was it, Aaron?

KAMRAN. What does he say?

JAMES. She left him for another woman.

I try the egg in my drink and it's sweet like fruit.

He thinks I've not heard.

KAMRAN. What?

JAMES. She didn't die when I was six. My dad threw her out. He lied.

KAMRAN. Shit.

JAMES. She died when I was ten. For those four years she was trying and failing to get me. Her and her partner, both. He says, she met her here.

KAMRAN. Sam. What do you say?

JAMES. I told him I needed the toilet.

KAMRAN. Did you?

JAMES. I didn't not.

I walk away. Ask two lads playing pool where they are and 'Through the back,' they both say. The men's. See two sinks, one stall. See helpline cards. Switchboard numbers and HIV. Graffiti.

Four years. It's all I can think and how, in them, I never saw her. How grieving broke every bone I own and it's back now like a rash… like he's just this second said… like I'm six again, seven again, eight again, nine.

I look for her face in my own at the mirror and remember, in order, these:

The smell of nail varnish remover.

Walks along to Moorclose Spar.

The theme tunes to her soaps.

SlimFast and Vosene.

Swearing like a docker.

Dancing sitting down.

Her fever for reading.

And forever always asking, 'how's your fettle, lad?'

I wish to see her one last time. If only to mention them all.

KAMRAN. And after that?

JAMES. I find a pint and a bag of Seabrooks at the bar.

KAMRAN. Where's Aaron?

JAMES. Selling raffle tickets. I make small talk with Diana Ross in his absence.

KAMRAN. What was her crack like?

JAMES. Supreme. There's a charity box on the bar top for a Retired Steelworkers Choir. On it a picture of Wendy's Tom. Uncle Tom.

KAMRAN. He wasn't lying.

JAMES. I send her a photo of it. Him singing his broken heart out with rows of other lads.

KAMRAN. It's best she knows.

JAMES. Aaron arrives with a tin of Monster and a sweat on.

AARON. The raffle's buggered. I've left Shania fishing the ticket book out of her Snakebite and black with half a left Twix and less hope. Be a love and blow on her, could you? She's burning the hell up.

JAMES. Shania Twain?

AARON. Me, you clown.

> JAMES *blows on* AARON.

And here's me thinking rock bottom was Lulu's wig. Greg, I said, you look like psoriasis, lose it. Better still, burn it. Madonna's in an Aldi bag in the boot of the Mazda Bongo, who cares, use her.

JAMES. Absolutely.

AARON. Are my eyebrows still on? It's my first time Avon micro fining.

JAMES. Two out of two.

AARON. That's nice. And you haven't any gaffer tape on you, have you?

JAMES. I wish he'd said that.

KAMRAN. What did he say?

JAMES. Two things. He was worried about his headline act.

KAMRAN. Why?

JAMES. He hadn't shown up.

KAMRAN. And?

JAMES. Did I wanna meet Sam?

KAMRAN. Did you?

JAMES. I didn't not.

AARON. I could send her over? Take you there? Whatever you think's best.

JAMES. **Send her here**, I say, and he's off.

> I watch him tell her. Him point and smile. Sam doesn't look. She sips her drink, says something to Kenickie and she's up.
>
> Incoming.
>
> I stare at the floor till I see trainers. Wondering if they're part of the costume. Hear her heart. Realise it's mine. She says my name.

SAM. **James.**

JAMES. Look up. **Alright?**

> She asks if I wanna drink.

SAM. **Do you wanna drink?**

JAMES. **I reckon I need a one**, I tell her and neck my existing pint.

> She orders. Smells of Tipp-Ex and wet-look hair gel.
>
> **Saw you in Tesco.**

SAM. **Saw you, too.**

JAMES. She says she's seen me loads. She's nervous. Both are.

SAM. **I've never been brave enough to talk to you.**

JAMES. **What made you tonight?**

SAM. **A bottle and a half of Cava in the flat.**

JAMES. **Where you lived with her?**

SAM. **Where I lived with her.**

JAMES. Sam stares at my face for the whole of 'A Little Respect'.

> She catches a cry and swallows it whole like a cobra.

SAM. **You look so like her.**

JAMES. **Were you with her when she died?**

SAM. **We're bypassing small talk then?**

JAMES. Were you?

SAM. **Fortunately. It was quick. She was comfortable.**

JAMES. **And you met her here?**

SAM. **My dad'd been a miner like hers. Your grandad. We got talking.**

JAMES. **About mining?**

SAM. **About family. And coal and steel and men. You know this whole area was the steelworks? All that remains is the pub.**

JAMES. **Why couldn't she have fought harder for me?**

SAM. **Your dad put up a very dirty fight.**

JAMES. I find myself hurting for a time I never had. For better lessons and less steel. I sit as I would've if they'd got to take me home and tell her bits about my life. Foods I like. Films I've seen. I say about Dad. How weak I am. How bad I let you down and how now everything's fucked.

KAMRAN. It's not.

JAMES. I tell her all sorts and it's disgusting – from the middles of my bones and out of my control – I dunno what I'm doing but it all just keeps on spilling – saying only how I'm ugly, how I'm broken, how I'm broke…

She asks what I do now. If I'm working or learning or…

SAM. **How's your fettle, lad?**

JAMES. I dunno what to say.

Eventually go, **do you know how Kamran eats pizza? Upside down.**

And in order to specifically remember something he specifically remembers something completely different. He's an idiot.

SAM. **Right.**

JAMES. **He's got an entire song about the periodic table.**

SAM. **Wow.**

JAMES. **No, not wow, Sam. I hate it. Hate him.**

SAM. **Who's Kamran?**

JAMES. **It's so annoying. No one makes me mad like him. Like I'm burning.**

He's my bonfire night. I'm his fireworks and he's my match. And he lights me like only he can and I go from gunpowder to colour so quick – so unexpected – that before I know it I'm fire. Ablaze.

KAMRAN. That's not anger.

JAMES. What is it?

KAMRAN. What does Sam say?

JAMES. That my mam's favourite drink was Archers and lemonade and should we have a double one each? Said too much.

KAMRAN. What's it like?

JAMES. Fizzy petrol.

She asks me to dance.

SAM. **Would you dance with me?**

JAMES *nods. They dance.*

JAMES. It's less of a dance floor and more just where the carpet's most worn. But room enough for her to hold me at the arms, me at hers and sway school-disco-slow. Aaron above us singing.

I stare at photos up the walls from the 80s, 90s and older. Pictures of love – of riots and fighting – this room, other rooms – tank tops, queens – and feel strong. Stronger than before. Feel solid. Feel handsome.

Sam was pretending she was dancing with mam – I felt it. Me with...

KAMRAN. Who?

JAMES. No one.

SAM. **I know him, you know.**

KAMRAN. She tells you. Sam tells you.

SAM. **Kamran. He's been here. Comes here. Centuries old and home to those the town spits out. It's a lighthouse for lads like him.**

They separate.

JAMES. The music stops. Steel taps the microphone with an announcement.

AARON. **I'm afraid our headline act for this evening.**

There's been an incident up at Gaslight.

He's alright... be more than alright... but if we could just...

JAMES. Disco lights dim and all we all hear is the crawl of the tide outside. It's spits and crashes. Rage and salt. The roar of a sea who's seen it all before.

23:26. Man down.

Silence.

I leave. Sprint two miles east to Stainburn.

KAMRAN. Mine?

JAMES. **23:44 and your mam answers.**

GITA. **Why are you here, James?**

JAMES. **I need to talk to him.**

GITA. **Too late.**

JAMES. **It's actually life or death.**

GITA. **He's took the dog out with his dad.**

JAMES. **At this hour?**

GITA. We know everything. We've had some very big conversations here tonight. Each, at some point, cried and all because of you – the million-quid kid.

JAMES. I lost it. I'm just James again. Which way did they go?

GITA. He tells me you're leaving. Well. Know this – the bits of you you don't like... or understand... you take with you wherever you go.

JAMES. I'm staying now. And it's a small town, I can't not see him.

GITA. We've had a some very big conversations here tonight.

JAMES. You've said.

GITA. My Arjun has a friend at a university. Assures us he can have his A-levels done in a single year there. After that, a degree.

JAMES. Where?

GITA. Far away. Where he'll think of you... and us... and this town, rarely... and then never. Go home, James.

JAMES. I could come in and wait? Won't touch nowt.

Silence.

GITA. You broke his heart and for that I could kill you. But you did it by letting him love you. By being handsome and boisterous... tender and idle... honest... tough.

By encouraging him to be his wild, wild self.

Allow yourself. And light up the night.

JAMES. I told her I wish I'd had a mam as good as her.

KAMRAN. And then you walked here. The end.

JAMES. And then I went home. The almost-end.

KAMRAN. What for?

JAMES. **23:56.** It's the last time I'll ask. You know him well enough to know what was said. He came with no surprises.

KAMRAN *thinks, nods.*

JAMES. **Dad?**

MARC. **James.**

JAMES. The house is a tip. I hear lads upstairs flipping drawers. See albums and Argos catalogues strewn across the floor. **What's happening?**

MARC. **Wendy said she'd heard neither hide nor hair from you.**

JAMES. **I've told you, we've looked, it's not here.**

MARC. **Worth a punt for a million.**

(*Shouts.*) **Owt yet, lads?**

JAMES. 'No,' they shout.

MARC. **Soon. Shame about that pint of ours. Me and you could've been great mates. Have put the world to rights over many a year yet.**

JAMES. **I met my Uncle Aaron.** He stops. Starts again. Finds a quid in the crease of the sofa and returns to his sideboard drawers. **Mam's brother.**

MARC. **I know who he is.**

JAMES. Finds Allen keys and tankard. Playing cards. Cluedo. **He introduced me to my mam's partner. Sam.**

MARC. **And is that a lad or a lass or an as-yet-unknown?**

JAMES. **Lass.**

MARC. **They'll've told you what happened.**

JAMES. **It was some lie.**

MARC. **I won't apologise.**

JAMES. **A mile away. For years. And you never said.**

MARC. **Does it matter?**

JAMES. **She was my mam.**

> He pulls down the drawbridge to the drinks cabinet. Swigs what's left of the Bacardi from my birthday. Watches himself in the mirror in its back.

MARC. **What matters… sunshine… is the re-opening of those steelworks.**

JAMES. Swig.

MARC. **I've the lads in the loft now looking and it's coming. We'll have such a bloody knees up and none of this'll matter.**

JAMES. Swig.

MARC. **You'll smell it in the air like the heydays. Sulphur and coal, you'll see it. Have a high street and a dance hall. Carnivals. Community.**

JAMES. Swig.

MARC. **Twenty years of trying to shift diesel from the beds of these nails. No need now. None. Did you see where my work boots went?**

JAMES. **You're wearing them.** Swig.

MARC. **Will I see about an apprenticeship for you?**

JAMES. **Why'd you do it?**

MARC. **They'll surely have some sort of training scheme.**

JAMES. **You sat and said about her funeral.**

MARC. **I'll ask.**

JAMES. **I was six. Where were you really?**

MARC. **Work your way up from stopper boy to Bessemer.**

JAMES. **Sat in the club with your mates?**

MARC. **Coke ovens, rolling mill, rail bank.**

JAMES. Laughing at me.

MARC. No.

JAMES. 'You'll never fucking guess what I've said.

What I've sat him on the edge of his bed and told...

He's heartbroken.

Obliterated.

His world in bits on his floor with his toys.'

MARC. You can stop that. Whining. They'll eat you alive.

JAMES. Who?

MARC. Lads on shift, going on like that.

JAMES. On what?

MARC. On shift. Your apprenticeship. Do you box?

JAMES. No.

MARC. We'll teach you. Unless you're happy sticking out? Seeming weak? Being defective, are you?

JAMES. Like my Uncle Aaron? Is that why I never met him?

MARC. We'll toughen you up yet.

JAMES. Why you kept me away from Mam?

MARC. I'll train you myself.

JAMES. Cos you thought it was catching?

MARC. Starting now. Hit me.

JAMES. No.

Silence.

You saw us on my birthday. Kamran said.

MARC. I saw you fighting.

JAMES. It's not a new thing.

MARC. **It's a start. And conflict's healthy – I bit a lad's ear off once.**

JAMES. Did you always know?

MARC. **Always. Hit me.**

  MARC *stares at* JAMES. *Silence.*

JAMES. Workington Man. Do you remember that? From the 2019 election. They said it meant Northern and old. Uneducated rugby fan. Had voted Brexit and might do Tory. You were outraged, remember?

'How dare they,' you said, 'boil so many men down to just one thing?' Something you are. Which, 'isn't uneducated, it's forgotten. It's failed. It's put out in the shallows in the dark and left to freeze.'

Don't boil me down to just one thing. That's not fair. And if you do, don't make it weak. Or defective. Or less than men like you.

Boil me down to love. And being in it. With him.

KAMRAN. What does he say?

JAMES. He tells that story about the seagull and the steelworks.

MARC. **We did things you'd be jailed for nowadays.**

JAMES. I let him. Wondering what – if anything – was ever true.

MARC. **Michael Swanny, the one that went to Jersey to be a comedian, I met him in the Bessemer cabin. He took a teacake out of his bait box. Took whatever was in it – let's say ham and cheese – out. And filled it with white powder.**

What you doing? I says. He says, watch this. So he opened the window and he broke it in half. Threw it out and this seagull come – swallowed it – went twelve foot and exploded.

I says, what the hell did you put in that? He says, soda ash – once it gets in the stomach and hits liquid, it explodes. He says, here, try it with that bit and handed me half.

We had no health and safety in those days. No need. Everyone looked after each other.

There were four thousand worked there when I did. Thirteen pubs down the Marsh and Quay alone – that's where I learnt to drink. And three canteens, which shows you how big it was.

The Steelworks closed here in '82. The last mine in '86. Ten years later, we had nothing. This town died with the yards. Left behind those mountains to rot. But we'll be back... you watch.

JAMES. No one's coming for you, Dad.

MARC (*chuckling*). This is on a site for protected birds mind.

Folk had only ever took.

Took the piss, took my job, took my... her.

And they'd've took you, too, if I hadn't.

Do you hate me, lad?

JAMES. No.

MARC. No.

JAMES. Midnight. Lads roll down the stairs with matching shaking heads.

'Soz, Marc,' they tell him in turn. 'Nowt.' **Too late anyway,** I tell them.

MARC. **Eh?**

JAMES. **We had it and we lost it.**

MARC. **How?**

JAMES. Kamran.

MARC. **Surprise, sur-fucking-prise. I told you.**

JAMES. **You told *him*. Every time you saw him.**

MARC. **What?**

JAMES. **You know what.**

MARC. **I don't like him. It's not racist.**

JAMES. **You are. And it stops now.**

> The lads know not to talk. They file out one by one to spark up their fags in the yard. Peel off into the night. Dad rolls his own and leans against the unit with what's left of the Bacardi. The end.
>
> I thought you'd gone.

KAMRAN. Come back, didn't I?

> Once Ted had said his piece, they're saying sudden others started. Folk expressing all sorts – ideas, wishes, confessions – like a cleanse.
>
> Wendy's suggested smashing the record for World's Biggest Bonfire, which apparently we set in 1993.

JAMES. Who's she's using as a guy?

KAMRAN. She wouldn't say but it's the lass from Moss Bay Chinese.

JAMES. Did you come for any other reason?

KAMRAN. To say goodbye.

JAMES. When you going?

KAMRAN. First thing.

JAMES. Right.

KAMRAN. And to tell you…

JAMES. What?

KAMRAN. When I threw it…

JAMES. Doesn't matter.

KAMRAN. I saw where it landed. You know how the Legion's got that dead-flat roof? I brought it back but you'd gone. Told my dad and it turns out his briefcase isn't only for old porn, it's for some of Sellafield's fattest deals.

JAMES. Your mam said you were walking the dog.

KAMRAN. We found Lynn and he negotiated you a little bit more than a million. Your final mile gives them 100% share so… they went higher.

JAMES. Two?

KAMRAN. Seven. It'll be in your Little Savers account in five working days.

JAMES. Cool.

And you're still going?

KAMRAN. Have to.

JAMES. Go.

KAMRAN. What you gonna do with it?

JAMES. Is this about your anorak?

KAMRAN. I've got more. All packed. Well?

JAMES (*thinks*). Dunno. Not as certain now. Suppose…

KAMRAN. They can't hear you.

JAMES *stands at the microphone and stares out.*

JAMES (*into mic*). I can see all the way to the fells.

JAMES *looks to* KAMRAN, *the audience,* KAMRAN, *the audience.*

(*Into mic.*) I hate the Lake District. How different it is for how close it is.

Try wandering as lonely as a single mam. As someone who can't pay their council tax bill. As those seven young lads my dad saw die.

(*Shouts.*) Beatrix Potter can go and fuck himself.

(*Into mic.*) It started with a Salterbeck kiss.

KAMRAN *exits.*

(*Into mic.*) And it's not the steelworks he misses, it's his community. It's needing thirteen pubs for four thousand thirsty mouths. It's coal and steel and men and love, it's people.

I'm glad mam lived before she died. That I've gained an uncle, and an auntie, in Aaron and even a something in Sam. Cos Kamran was right. There's joy in being different, muck can shimmer and what home means can change – we can change.

It's not the steelworks you miss, it's each other. But look at you. The town we thought dead – it lives.

Melt us in the furnace, burn us and convert us. Blow out all impurities and re-cast folk anew. Rewind. Rewire. Rush us through the crucible and roll us out afresh. From pig iron to steel. Before to now. Yesterday to today. Transform.

Be each other's bonfires and light up every night.

I'm buying the pub. Centuries old and home to those the town spits out. It's a lighthouse for lads like me. The rest you can have. Don't want it.

Want him.

Where is he?

My wild, wild boy.

JAMES *scans the crowd.*

I watch Wendy handing out carnations for heroes.

(*Shouts.*) Kamran?

Watch Nick find his mam in the crowd.

(*Louder.*) Where are you?

Watch Kelly and the baby come.

(*Louder.*) Come back.

The Retired Steelworkers Choir and a chorus of drag queens file out.

Watch them watch Tom and his choir file out.

Aaron and his chorus of queens.

Not yet. No. I'm not ready.

JAMES *stares out.*

(*Into mic.*) Scafell Pike. Scafell. Helvellyn. Skiddaw. Great End.

(*Louder.*) Surrender, surrender, heart says, go.

(*Shouts.*) Don't go.

KAMRAN *appears.*

KAMRAN. What you shouting about?

JAMES. Nervous.

KAMRAN. Me, too.

JAMES. I love you.

KAMRAN. I love you, too.

JAMES. Shame you've gotta go.

KAMRAN. Come.

JAMES. Aye?

KAMRAN. How quick can you be ready?

JAMES. Ready now.

KAMRAN. And it ends with a Salterbeck kiss.

They kiss. The choir and the chorus sing.

CHOIR/CHORUS (*singing*).
   The hum of something coming
   The fizz of a working men's club sign
   There's something in the water
   As twelve-hour shifts approach home time

The chip shop chitter chatter
The rumour mill's right about this crowd
There's music in the river
As Uppies & Downies all call out

'You can see the Lakes out there, some say
But give me the Solway any day'

Make a noise, they say
Make a roar, they say
Sing it louder, prouder and make it what they say, come on
What they say, come on
Take a spark, they say
Make a mark, they say
Sing it louder, prouder and make it what they say, come on
What they say, come on

The clatter of a family
The march of a majorette squadron
The buzzing of the slag bank
There's lads in the stands singing new songs

'You can see the Lakes out there, some say
But give me the Solway any day'

Make a noise, they say
Make a roar, they say
Sing it louder, prouder and make it what they say, come on

What they say, come on
Take a spark, they say
Make a mark, they say
Sing it louder, prouder and make it what they say, come on
What they say

Watch the working men's club sing their song
Want that feeling I feel I belong
Watch the steelworking marras still grin
Watch them open their whole hearts to sing

Make a noise, they say
Make a roar, they say

Sing it louder, prouder and make it what they say, come on
What they say, come on
Take a spark, they say
Make a mark, they say
Sing it louder, prouder and make it what they say, come on
What they say, come on

End.

A Nick Hern Book

Steel first published in Great Britain as a paperback original in 2024 by Nick Hern Books Limited, The Glasshouse, 49a Goldhawk Road, London W12 8QP, in association with The Theatre by the Lake, Keswick

Steel copyright © 2024 Lee Mattinson

Lee Mattinson has asserted his right to be identified as the author of this work

Cover photography by Grant Archer

Designed and typeset by Nick Hern Books, London
Printed in Great Britain by Mimeo Ltd, Huntingdon, Cambridgeshire PE29 6XX

A CIP catalogue record for this book is available from the British Library

ISBN 978 1 83904 408 3

CAUTION All rights whatsoever in this play are strictly reserved. Requests to reproduce the text in whole or in part should be addressed to the publisher.

Amateur Performing Rights Applications for performance, including readings and excerpts, by amateurs in the English language should be addressed to the Performing Rights Manager, Nick Hern Books, The Glasshouse, 49a Goldhawk Road, London W12 8QP, *tel* +44 (0)20 8749 4953, *email* rights@nickhernbooks.co.uk, except as follows:

Australia: ORiGiN Theatrical, *tel* +61 (2) 8514 5201,
email enquiries@originmusic.com.au, *web* www.origintheatrical.com.au

New Zealand: Play Bureau, 20 Rua Street, Mangapapa, Gisborne 4010,
tel +64 21 258 3998, *email* info@playbureau.com

Professional Performing Rights Rights Applications for performance by professionals in any medium and in any language throughout the world should be addressed in the first instance to Nick Hern Books, see contact details above.

No performance of any kind may be given unless a licence has been obtained. Applications should be made before rehearsals begin. Publication of this play does not necessarily indicate its availability for amateur performance.

www.nickhernbooks.co.uk/environmental-policy

www.nickhernbooks.co.uk

facebook.com/nickhernbooks

twitter.com/nickhernbooks